IMAGES
of America

Fort Worth's Historic Hotels

On the Cover: Pictured is downtown Fort Worth at Main and Seventh Streets looking north. (Courtesy Jack White Photograph Collection, Special Collections, UTA.)

IMAGES
of America

Fort Worth's Historic Hotels

Simone C. De Santiago Ramos

ARCADIA
PUBLISHING

ISBN 978-0-7385-9974-8
Published by Arcadia Publishing
Charleston, South Carolina

Printed in the United States of America

Library of Congress Control Number: 2013937877

For all general information, please contact Arcadia Publishing:
Telephone 843-853-2070
Fax 843-853-0044
E-mail sales@arcadiapublishing.com
For customer service and orders:
Toll-Free 1-888-313-2665

Visit us on the Internet at www.arcadiapublishing.com

To my grandfather Albert, chef and hotelier extraordinaire

Contents

ACKNOWLEDGMENTS

With a background in the hospitality industry and a love for local history, I was delighted to write a book that combined these two fields. However, it would not have been possible without all the help I received while undertaking this project.

I would like to thank the following individuals and organizations that helped complete this endeavor: John Avila, CEO of Thos. S. Byrne Construction; the North Fort Worth Historical Society; Betty Shankle from the Fort Worth Public Library, Genealogy History and Archives Unit (FTWPL); Dawn Youngblood at the Tarrant County Archives; Cathy Spitzenberger and her staff at the Special Collections Library at the University of Texas in Arlington (UTA); Tom Shelton from UTSA; John Zak from the *Dallas Morning News*; David A. Matthews; and David Holt, NARA branch office, Fort Worth.

I benefited from the advice of Ann Sumerour, Fayetteville State University, and her valuable input and encouragement throughout this project. I would like to thank Katja Wright for accompanying me on some of the research trips, and Devon Gerlach for her technical support. I consider myself fortunate to work under professors Dr. Mike Campbell and Dr. Robert Citino, University of North Texas, and would like to show my gratitude to them.

I am further deeply indebted to Laura Bruns from Arcadia Publishing for her help and patience in this project.

Introduction

Fort Worth, originally named Camp Worth, was founded as a US Army outpost in 1849 on a bluff overlooking the Trinity River. The site was about 75 miles south of the Red River in North Texas, an almost equal distance to the Pacific and Atlantic Oceans. When the military relocated and abandoned the camp, civilians moved into the space. Although the city experienced some economic problems, the population steadily increased until the Civil War. During the war, the city's residents dwindled to a few hundred females but regained its population soon thereafter. Fort Worth developed into a bustling stop on the famous Chisholm cattle trail in the 1860s and 1870s. Hotels were nonexistent; cowboys stayed in boardinghouses or in rooms above the many saloons in town. Few establishments had bath facilities. A general bathhouse, however, was operating at that time in the city. In the early 1870s, it was announced that the city would be connected to the rail. In anticipation of the railroad's arrival and the expected boom in lodging facilities, city leaders in 1873 saw it necessary to set license fees for hotels at $12.50 and $7.50 for boardinghouses.

The population had grown dramatically, to 2,500 households, when, in July 1876, the Texas & Pacific Railroad arrived. Investors and hotel entrepreneurs both saw the need for better lodging facilities. By the end of the century, several hotels were built in Fort Worth. Hoteliers prided themselves on offering the latest comfort. The El Paso hotel, the first truly "big" house, was completed in 1877. Some of these hotels became symbols of prosperity, encompassing all the luxuries travelers would expect from elegant European hotels. Fort Worth itself was expanding, too. New structures in the city included a city courthouse, a prison, a much-needed fire station, and a city hall. In the mid-1880s, boarders could expect to pay between $5 and $10 a week at most places, while a stop at the bathhouse set the traveler back 25¢. In 1878, there were 10 hotels operating in the city, including the Cosmopolitan, the US Hotel, and the European Hotel Restaurant & Saloon, run by J.F. Woodward. He caused a small sensation when he introduced female wait staff to his establishment. In order to keep up with the European standard, early entrepreneurs hired European-born and -trained staff for both the front and back of the house. In January 1915, the Fort Worth Hotel and Restaurant Keepers Association was founded, and the hotel greeters in the city joined the Hotel Greeters Association of America in 1917. The rise of the stockyards and meat-packaging plants just north of the city limits stimulated the economy further, and in 1908, the Northside Coliseum was built to house the Southwestern Exposition and Fat Stock Show (later renamed the Southwestern Exposition and Livestock Show). Electrical railcars had made their debut a few years earlier within city limits, and by 1916, the city had laid 66 miles of track.

The city experienced an economic boom in the 1920s, when oil was found in the area. That new wealth was reflected in the many luxury hotels that were added to the landscape. By 1926, Fort Worth had 61 hotels within the city limits. Some hotels were known for their exquisite restaurants and food, while others offered nightclubs and live entertainment. Guests from all over the world enjoyed their stay in the city. As with most places in the United States and around the world, the prosperity came to an end in 1929 and did not return until after World War II. New faces and businesses showed up in town when the military moved into the city and established several training grounds. After the war, the city became the second largest aircraft production center in America and was, in the late 1950s, the region with the most active oil wells in the world. But the decades between 1940 and 1960 were largely overshadowed by war, followed by the return of the soldiers. The Cold War also affected the city and the lodging industry. New concepts, such as motor lodges, accommodated the ever-growing number of travelers on the road. And still more changes took place in the late 1950s with the introduction and expansion of air travel.

This book is organized in the chronological order of the properties built. The first chapter, "Birth of Fort Worth's Hotel Industry," covers the time period from the first lodging establishment to the turn of the 20th century. "Growth of the City" includes the heyday of the cattle barons and the rise of the first lavish, luxury places. Because of America's involvement in the World War I, the US Army established Camp Bowie in the Arlington Heights area, which trained 100,000 men. The Army Air Force converted three airfields into centers of aviation training, investing heavily in this new technology. The "Oil Boom and Great Depression" is the title of the third chapter. By 1920, the cattle barons were replaced with oil barons, who demanded more luxury hotels and first-class accommodations. Many oil barons established headquarters in the city and saw a need for elegant hotels, lodging, and meeting facilities to entertain their clients and conduct business. By then, the city was also the leading grain market in the southwestern United States and operated the largest cold-storage facilities. Among the celebrities that stayed over the decades in Fort Worth were Hollywood legends, mobsters, and politicians. "War and the Rise of the Automobile" discusses the implications of World War II and the boom in highway travel that followed in the 1950s. Five major highways crossed the city, which furthered the expansion of a new concept: motor lodges and motels. The last chapter, with the fitting title "Urban Decay and Renewal," looks at the problems these older properties presented to the city and the questions of demolition and preservation. Two of the oldest and still-operating hotels, the Texas and Blackstone, are discussed in more depth. The Blackstone in particular is featured, with its glorious past, the many years the hotel stood empty, and its resurrection. It reflects the good times but also the bad times and the ups and downs Fort Worth as a city has experienced.

One

Birth of Fort Worth's Hotel Industry 1854–1900

Fort Worth's hotel industry was born in 1854, when Capt. Ephraim M. Daggett converted an old US Army stable on the northwest corner of the parade grounds into a hotel. Just five years earlier, in May 1849, Maj. Ripley A. Arnold of the US Dragoons had established a temporary Army outpost near the West Fork of the Trinity River. By November 1853, however, the troops had left the campsite. Captain Daggett eventually sold the small hotel to Lawrence Steel, who renamed it Steele's Tavern. Steele is considered one of the city's pioneers, having been in Texas since 1839 and in Fort Worth since 1854. After he sold his place, it was renamed Andrew's Tavern.

Railroad representatives visited Fort Worth in June 1872 to discuss the extension of the rail line into the city. In 1874, the city was incorporated and the first telegraph lines installed. In September, however, an economic depression halted rail expansion, and the population declined sharply. Businesses, including hotels and boardinghouses, closed, many for good. All changed, however, when, on July 18, 1876, the long-awaited railroad arrived.

Meals at that time sold for 25¢ a plate, and the European Hotel & Restaurant, located at Third and Houston Streets, advertised that guests "got what they want and pay for only that." In the early 1880s, visitors could choose between the City Hotel, Junction House, Plaza, Sprague House, the Waterman, or the Faires' Hotel & Dining Parlor. More lodging facilities, with names like Germania House, El Paso Hotel, the Ginocchio Hotel, the Globe, the Grand Central, and the Hotel Da Louvre, opened their doors to receive travelers. The First Stockyard Hotel & Exchange was opened in 1885. The end of the century saw hotels such as the Brewery Exchange Hotel, the San Antonio Exchange, the Spring Palace Hotel, and the Metropolitan offering their services. Local hotel proprietors and investors included John Scharbauer, Winfield Scott, and J.W. Bicknell. Many early and successful hoteliers in Fort Worth were women. Mrs. M.L. Trimmler and Lina Dunn owned the Mansion, Ann and Nellie Clark operated the Clark House, a Mrs. Moors ran the Hotel Harrald, and a Mrs. Sargent operated the Tremont Hotel.

This 1940s drawing shows Camp Worth, situated on a bluff overlooking the Trinity River. After the withdrawal of the military, one of the stables was converted into Fort Worth's first hotel. (Courtesy Jack White Photograph Collection, Special Collections, UTA.)

The only remnant from Fort Worth's first hotel is Steele's Bell. The bell, cast in London in 1782, was used as a "soup's on" signal in the lodging place. Steele eventually sold the place to Albert Andrews of Kentucky, who renamed it Andrew's Tavern. Steele than built the Transcontinental Hotel. The bell was donated in 1871 to the Moslah Temple in Fort Worth, where Lawrence Steel was a member. (Author's photograph.)

This is a portrait of Capt. Ephraim M. Daggett, Fort Worth's first hotelier. (Courtesy Fort Worth City Directory.)

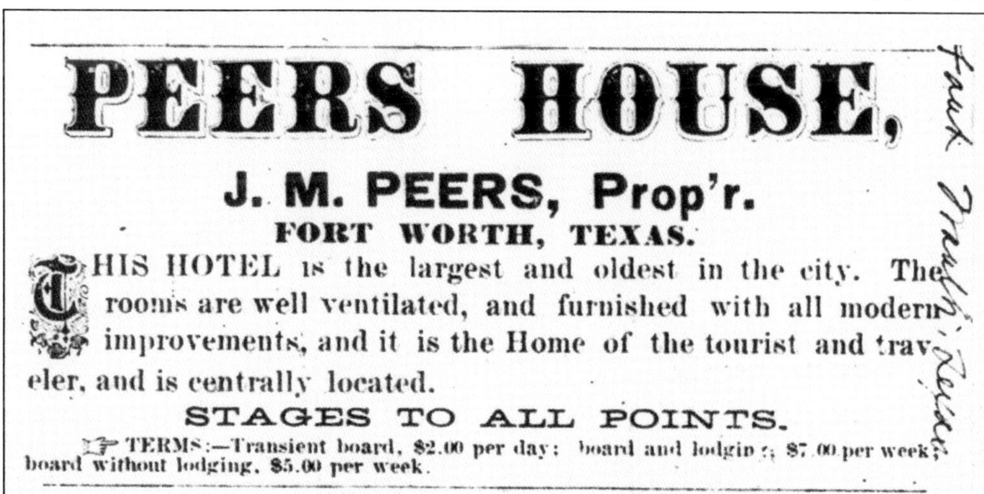

PEERS HOUSE,

J. M. PEERS, Prop'r.

FORT WORTH, TEXAS.

THIS HOTEL is the largest and oldest in the city. The rooms are well ventilated, and furnished with all modern improvements, and it is the Home of the tourist and traveler, and is centrally located.

STAGES TO ALL POINTS.

TERMS:—Transient board, $2.00 per day; board and lodging, $7.00 per week; board without lodging, $5.00 per week.

Gen. Joseph M. Peers, originally from Richmond, Virginia, operated the Virginia House in 1873. At the time, this was considered the largest establishment in Fort Worth. The general became the sole proprietor of the Peers House in 1876, considered the best house in North Texas. Peers House, advertised as being a large house with good water and neat and well-furnished rooms, was located on Fifth and Rusk Streets. (Courtesy Fort Worth City Directory.)

This 1870s photograph shows the Fort Worth Denver City House (at left), which offered meals and lodging, and the Hutchison Hotel (at right). This complex was located on Jones and Fifteenth Streets. (Courtesy *Fort Worth Star Telegram* Collection, UTA.)

This 1888 photograph shows the Georgia House, a two-story brick building located at 1110 Houston Street. F. Prickett was the proprietor, and he shared the building with Hicks Groceries. (Courtesy UTA.)

The El Paso Hotel, which opened in March 1878, was one of the finest hotels in the state. It is considered to be the earliest grand hotel in the city. This three-story brick building, located on the northwest corner of Fourth and Main Streets, contained 80 rooms and advertised all new furniture. It was originally run by the legendary hotelier Maj. Cyrus King Fairfax, followed by John P. Alexander and Mrs. H.N. Humphreys. The cost to build the El Paso was $25,000. The hotel offered, for the convenience of its guests, wood plank sidewalks. In 1885, the El Paso was renovated and renamed the Pickwick Hotel. (Courtesy Fort Worth Public Library.)

The two-story Clark House, located on Main and Lancaster Streets near the Texas & Pacific depot, was managed by the female team of Mrs. E. Bennett and Anne and Nellie Clark. It opened in 1875 but was no longer in operation after 1886.

In December 1885, Comanche chief Quanah Parker and his uncle Yellow Bear stayed in the Pickwick Hotel. By accident, gas escaped from a lantern during the night and Yellow Bear died from asphyxiation in the hotel. Parker himself barely escaped with his life. By 1888, the Pickwick was owned by W.B. Wells and managed by W.E. Kennedy.

This Pickwick menu is from Thanksgiving 1888. The meal featured French-inspired dishes, such as fillets of striped bass à la Normandy and pomme de terre en bouclée.

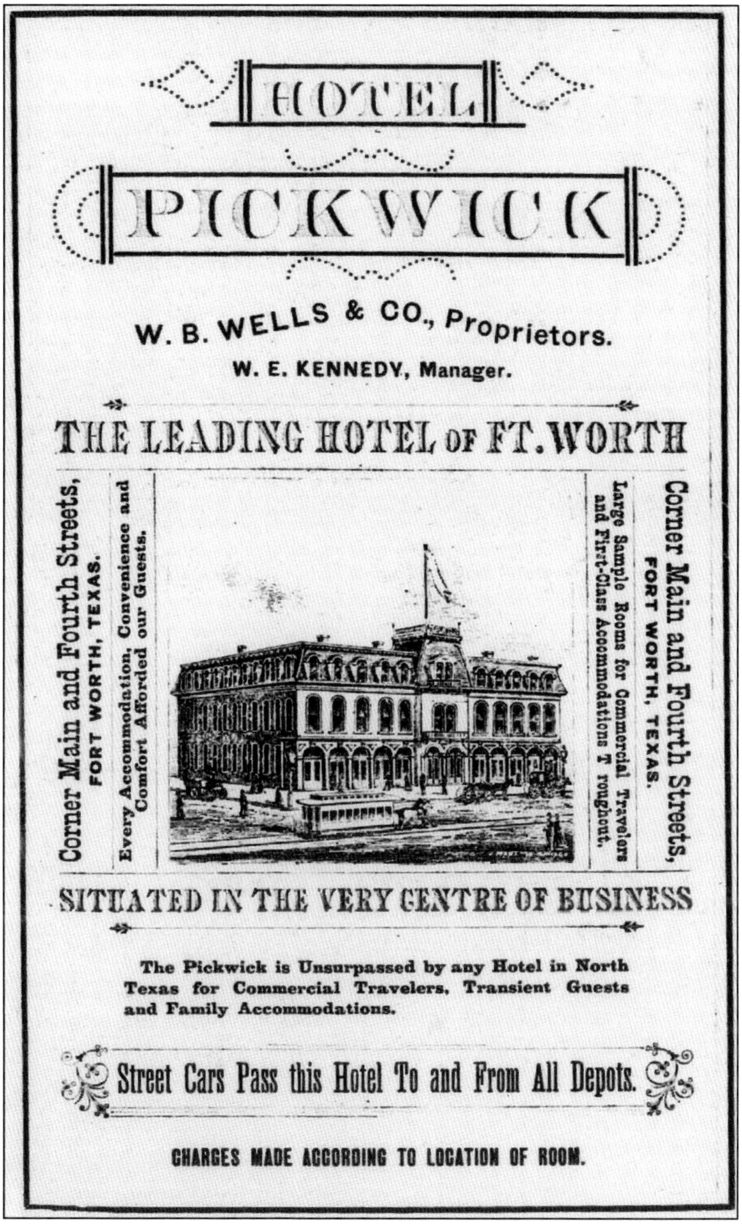

By the early 1890s, the Pickwick Hotel had been renovated, and it reopened under a new name: the Delaware Hotel. The hotel was now owned by M.C. Harley and Jerome Roche but was eventually sold to the McLean & Mudge hotel company in February 1895. Yet, less than two years later, in January 1897, it again changed hands when Ernest M. Maupin and the Delaware Hotel Co. became the sole proprietor. The Delaware operated exclusively on the European plan, which does not include any meals. By 1909, the hotel's facade underwent renovation. A portico stretching alongside Main Street was erected, but the city requested its removal for safety reasons. By 1910, the management of the Delaware announced plans to erect a 10-story hotel on Houston Street between Fourth and Fifth Streets and to connect and extend the properties by porticos. The Delaware was affiliated with Ben Tillar's father, who later built the Westbrook Hotel. (Courtesy Fort Worth Public Library.)

This photograph shows the hotel without the portico. Although the Delaware was still considered one of the finest addresses in the city, guests complained about the hotel's problem with mosquitoes. One guest, having been kept awake all night, recalled that the insects were so bad that he rather walked the streets at night. (Courtesy UTA.)

This view of downtown Fort Worth dates to the 1890s. The Randal House, one of the smaller lodging establishments in the city, can be seen on the left side across from Schober's Market. The Randal House is the smalled building tucked behind J.H. Carter Groceries. (Courtesy UTA.)

The three-story brick building of the Waterman Hotel was conveniently located on the corner of Main and Eleventh Streets and was served by the mule-drawn streetcars. The hotel was built by Joel Waterman. By 1886, he sold it to C.E. George. It was eventually renamed Spring Palace and was associated with the Texas Spring Palace.

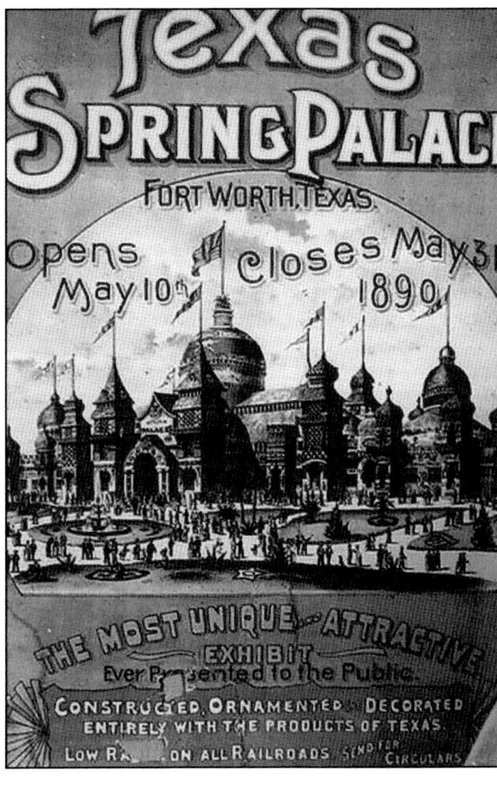

The original Texas Spring Palace opened in May 1889 to attract settlers to North Texas. The palace itself, which had no lodging facility attached to it, burned down at the end of its second season, on May 30, 1890. The city had plans to rebuild it but was unable to get enough investors onboard. The Spring Palace Hotel burned to the ground in 1895.

The Ellis Hotel was built by James Franklin Ellis, one of the first civilian settlers of the area, in 1885 for $140,000. The hotel, managed by famed chef Edward Mueller and S. Fort, was considered the city's social center for years. The Ellis was located on Second, Third, and Throckmorton Streets. The four-story brick structure offered the latest in luxury, including the first passenger and freight elevators, electric lights, and steam-heated rooms in the South. The hotel had a three-story brick annex and was served by the one-mule street trolley. Famous artist Frederic Remington stayed in the hotel during his visits to Fort Worth. A fast-spreading kitchen fire burned the Ellis and the big produce house of Garlington & Montgomery on September 21, 1891. It was reported that the Ellis Hotel was worth $60,000, and its furniture was valued at $25,000. (Courtesy UTA.)

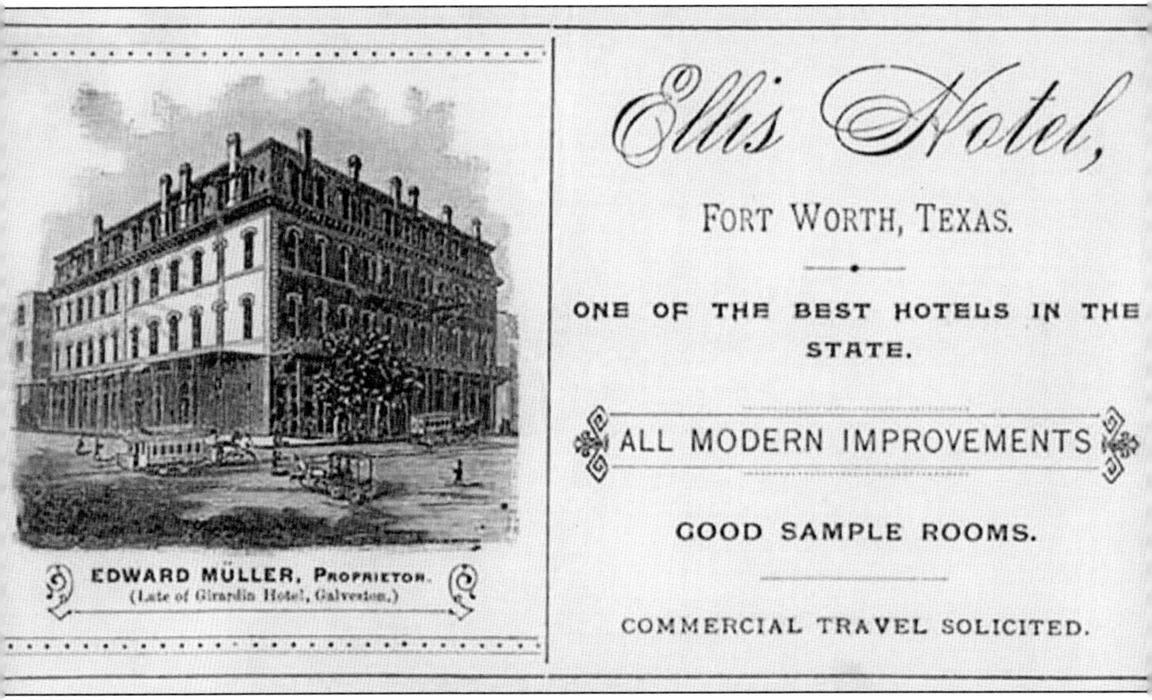

This advertisement describes the Ellis Hotel as one of the best hotels in the state. The accompanying image shows mule-drawn streetcars in front of the hotel.

The Mansion Hotel was built in 1876 with the arrival of the railway. Served by streetcars, it was conveniently located within walking distance to the post office, telegraph station, and the newly erected opera house. The hotel offered 95 rooms and could seat 150 guests in the dining room. The Mansion, located on Fourth and Rusk Streets, offered room rates ranging from $2 to $2.50 a night. It was operated by W.W. Dunn and his wife, Lina, and later by their son B.H. Dunn. Although the Mansion had a nice, large dining room (below), it was still supported by columns in the middle, making the room unpractical for large gatherings or dances.

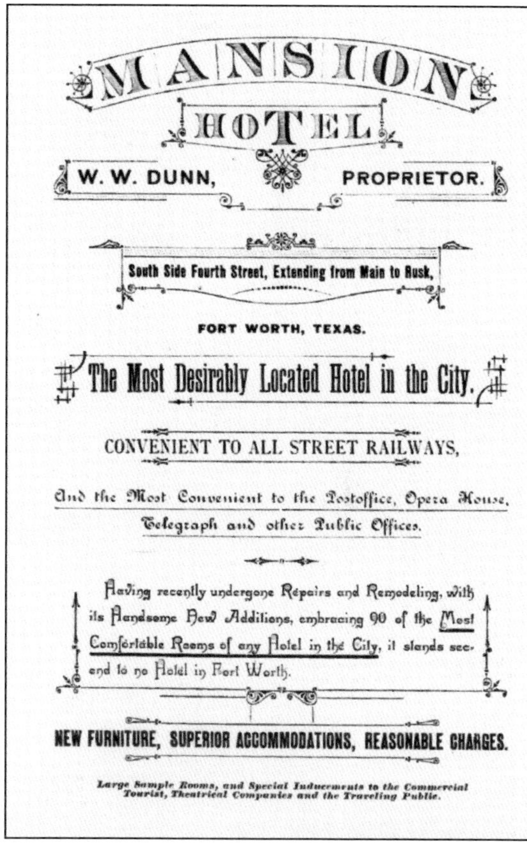

Dunn's Mansion Garage on Commerce Street was built in 1924 on the former site of the Mansion Hotel to accommodate the growing number of cars in Fort Worth. In 1935, three more stories were added. The Mansion Garage was converted into office space starting in the 1990s. This photograph shows the Mansion Garage (right) with the Texas & Pacific station in the background.

THE NEW
MANSION HOTEL

RATES $1.50 PER DAY AND NOT ONE PENNY MORE.
GUESTS STOPPING BY WEEK OR MONTH WILL BE GIVEN SPECIAL RATES.
YOU ARE INVITED TO SEEK HOTEL ACCOMODATIONS AT THE MANSION.

GEO. D. KOENIG, Propr.
"KING DODO"

THE MANSION IS NOW ONE OF THE BEST REASONABLE PRICED (and home-like) HOTELS IN FT. WORTH, AND PROPOSES TO GROW BETTER AS THE DAYS GO BY.

OFFICE ON EAST FOURTH STREET, BETWEEN MAIN and RUSK.

SPECIAL RATES TO THEATRICAL PEOPLE AND TRAVELING PARTIES.

By 1905, George Koenig (or, as he called himself, "King Dodo") managed the Mansion property. In order to compete with the other establishments in town, Koenig targeted the "theatrical people and travelling parties." However, by 1909, the hotel had changed management for the third time in six years. Although still operating under the American plan, the hotel had raised its rate to $2 a night. In late December 1920, both the Mansion and Grammer Hotels burned to the ground in the so-called Big Blaze, which caused property damage of $200,000.

The Hotel Harrold, seen at left in the above photograph, was located at 1102 Houston Street and was managed by a Mrs. Moore. The photograph shows the Carnival of Flowers parade in 1897 in front of the hotel. The Hotel de Mason was operated by Thomas Mason, who previously worked as headwaiter at the Mansion Hotel before operating his own place at 607 Rusk Street, between Fifth and Sixth Streets. The photograph below shows guests in the Mason's restaurant. (Courtesy UTA.)

The Ye Old Arlington Inn, a 123-room resort, was built in the summer of 1891 in Arlington Heights by millionaire developers McLean and H.B. Chamberlain. The construction of the hotel, at an estimated cost of $100,000, was announced with great fanfare in the local press. The inn was affiliated with the Lake Como resort and was served by streetcars to the city. The first floor was built of Pecos stone, while the other three stories were constructed of pine. This resort inn burned down in November 1894 and was never rebuilt. The Ye Old Inn is often confused with the Grand Arlington Hotel, a three-story wooden structure built in 1888 by a Mr. Johnson and located at Eleventh and Houston Streets. In October 1889, the so-called Big Fire of Fort Worth broke out at the feed and livery stable of Young & Kouhne on Houston Street and consumed several smaller boardinghouses and the Grand Arlington Hotel. (Courtesy Fort Worth Public Library.)

The Fort Worth Stock Yard Hotel and Exchange, located in North Fort Worth, was built in 1885. The complex was demolished in March 1902 to make way for the Swift & Company packing plant. In this mid-1880s photograph, cattlemen proudly show off their livestock. (Courtesy of the North Fort Worth Historical Society.)

The three-story brick Richelieu Hotel at 1415 Main Street and Fifteenth Street was, in the late 1890s, considered one of the better accommodations in the city. Jim Mellown was able to charge $2 a day in 1898. The hotel advertised itself as the "only first-class trade accommodation" but did not yet offer any amenities, like telephones, to its guests. By 1900, J.B. Sprinkle, a Fort Worth policeman turned hotelier, owned the Richelieu. The room rate had dropped to $1.50, and in 1909, the Richelieu had adopted both the American and European plans for the convenience of its guests. Just four years later, in May 1913, city inspector Charles Allen condemned the property. Eventually, the building was purchased by Winfield Scott's widow as an investment property. (Courtesy Fort Worth City Directory.)

The Metropolitan Hotel was built in 1889 as "the only European hotel" by early hotel entrepreneur Winfield Scott. The hotel, known by the locals as the Met, was located on Main and Eighth Streets. Each room had a window and hot water. The Metropolitan Hotel was originally planned as a five-story building, but it was only erected as a three-story brick structure. In 1908, plans were drawn up to enlarge parts of the hotel and add seven floors facing Main Street, but, eventually, only two more were added. The Metropolitan underwent several updates and renovations during its time in business. After an extended renovation of more than $250,000, each room had a telephone and baths were added to 65 rooms, for a total of 157 baths in the hotel. The Met offered a separate entrance and lobby, decorated in green Georgia marble, for ladies. (Courtesy UTA.)

The Great Banquet Room at the Metropolitan was located on the fourth floor. It was the largest single room of its kind in any hotel in Texas at the time. The construction was such that no pillar or column obstructed the view, making the space ideal for large gatherings and dances. It became one of the most popular places for social events. (Author's postcard.)

This view of the Metropolitan includes, on the roof, its own water tower. (Courtesy Tarrant County Archives, TCA.)

In this 1909 photograph of Main and Ninth Streets in Fort Worth, the Metropolitan Hotel is in the foreground at right. One block farther down is the Hotel Worth. In the spring of 1907, a 42-foot veranda was added over the Metropolitan's entrance and was used as an open-air parlor. At the same time, the hotel added a freight elevator for supplies and guest luggage. (Author's postcard.)

The Metropolitan lost its shine in the 1920s and 1930s, especially after the Blackstone and Texas opened. The hotel was sold to the Milner Hotel Company in 1938. A 1943 fire caused $39,000 in damages on the second floor. This photograph shows the hotel with the Milner sign in 1956. (Author's postcard.)

This photograph shows the Milner Hotel (center) in the summer of 1956 in the shadow of the Hotel Texas. The hotel was torn down in 1959 to make space for a parking lot for the adjacent Hotel Texas. It was in this parking lot that John F. Kennedy gave his final speech on the morning of his assassination. (Courtesy A. Davis Co, W.D. Smith, UTA.)

Originally owned and managed by Hermann Eberling, the Southern Hotel was one of the premier landmark hotels in the 1880s. The Southern was a three-story building located on Jones Street between Fourteenth and Fifteenth Streets, opposite the Santa Fe Station. By 1909, though, the glory days of the 15-room facility were over, and the hotel was mainly frequented by railroad laborers who worked at night and slept during the day. In January 1909, a gasoline-operated coffee urn exploded in the lunchroom and quickly developed into a raging inferno. The old, dry muslin walls aided in the fire and four guests died in the blaze. Although the Southern Hotel did not completely burn down, it sustained extensive property damage and was eventually torn down. (Courtesy Fort Worth City Directory.)

The Natatorium, sometimes called "The Nat," was built in 1890, when many smaller hotels and private homes had no baths. It featured a 95-foot swimming pool. The Rococo-style Natatorium and hotel was located at the southwest corner of East Third and Rusk (now Commerce) Streets. It offered Turkish and Russian baths, and out-of-town guests could rent rooms on the upper floors. The hotel was managed by Rufus M. Colgin. (Both, courtesy Forth Worth City Directory.)

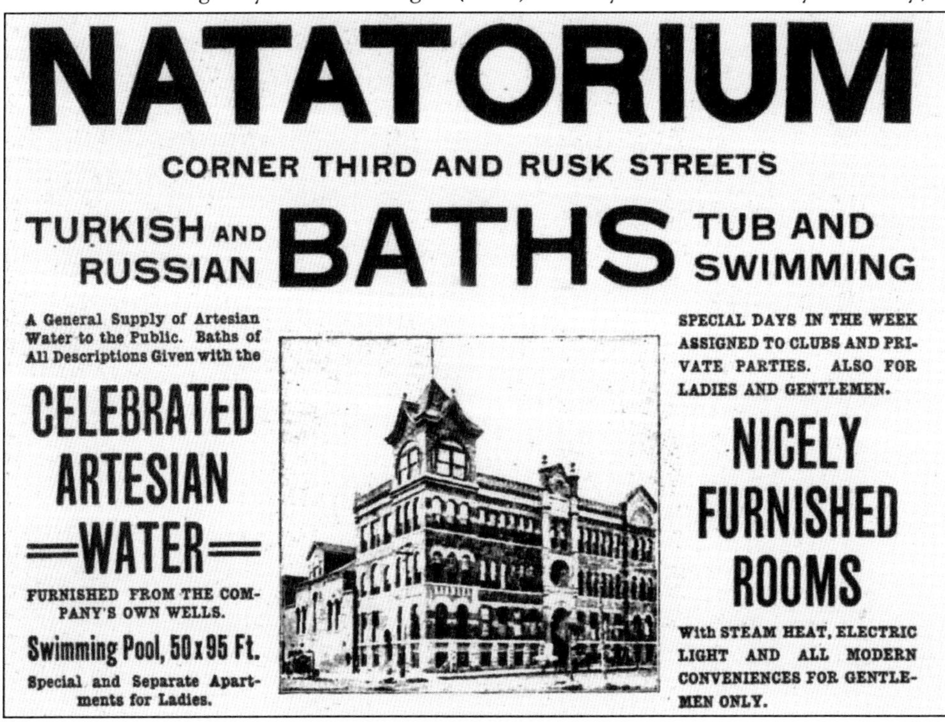

This drawing depicts the building that later became the first Hotel Worth. It was designed by Marshal Sanguinet for Judge George Hendricks around 1889 as an office building. By early 1891, voices in Fort Worth called for a grand, first-class hotel that would be second to none in Texas. In April 1891, renovation began on the existing structure. The Hotel Worth featured 132 all-window rooms and was located at Main and Seventh Streets. Hastily opened in November 1894 by cattle baron John Scharbauer and entrepreneur W.C. Stonestreet, this five-story hotel housed the August department store on the ground floor. Although the hotel was not completely finished at the time of the opening, the Hotel Worth was immediately booked up, since both the Pickwick and the Mansion were closed for remodeling. Three days after the Worth opened, the Ye Old Arlington Inn burned to the ground, and for several weeks, the Worth was the only luxury establishment in the city. It was managed by W.P. Hardwick until his death in 1902. To make way for the new Hotel Texas, part of the original Hotel Worth was torn down in 1920. In September 1922, the old Hotel Worth was converted back into an office building, (Courtesy FTWPL.)

During the Spanish-American War, hotel guests included Army officers who stayed in town while they purchased horses for the Army at the stockyards. This 1908 photograph shows the five-story Hotel Worth with its three-story annex on the right. The Worth occupied the east side of Main Street between Seventh and Eighth Streets. It eventually operated on the American plan. The August department store occupied the street-level floor on Main Street. Sam Avarello, an immigrant from Sicily, operated the shoe-shine stand for many decades in the lobby of the Hotel Worth. In 1902, the Worth was the first and largest hotel in the United States to include a telegraph substation, or so-called exchange, installed on the roof. This made it possible to have pay phones on each floor and two phone booths in the lobby for the convenience of the traveling public. But with the arrival of newer hotels in the city, the Hotel Worth declined in the second decade of the 20th century, changing hands and management several times. (Courtesy FTWPL.)

This is an advertisement for the Hotel Worth and the White Elephant Saloon and Restaurant from 1895. Both establishments were owned or partially owned by Winfield Scott. Here, the hotel is primarily advertising to male customers, as is evident by the billiard parlor notice. Jake Washer of Washer Brothers was the first guest in the Hotel Worth's dining room when it opened its doors to the public. He kept the same table until he got married. By the summer of 1910, the hotel started to market to women, advertising a women's luncheon, served at noon "to a most moderate price."

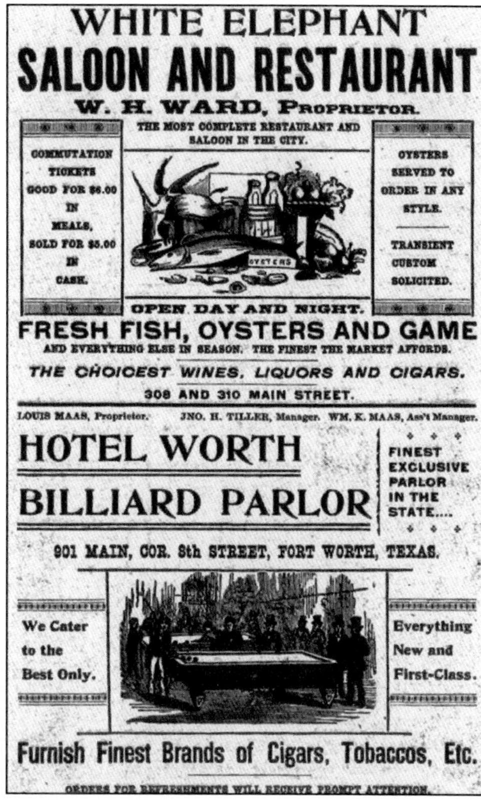

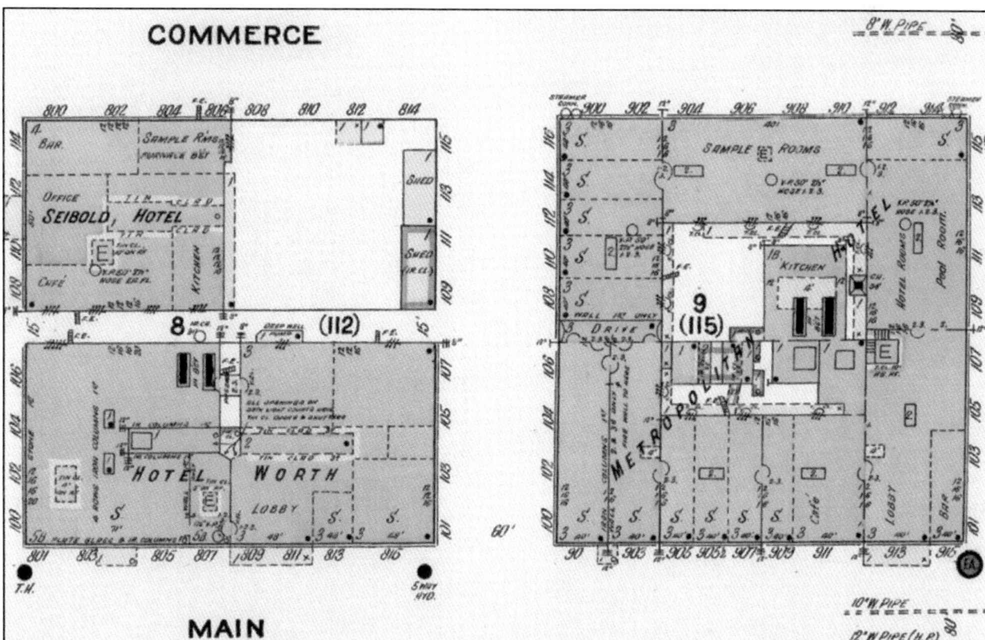

This 1911 Sandborn map shows the Hotel Worth in relation to the Metropolitan Hotel on Main Street and the Seibold Hotel on Commerce Street. (Courtesy Perry-Castaneda Library Collection, UT Austin.)

By October 1908, the five-story hotel and its annex were purchased by Winfield Scott for $250,000 from two Houston investors who had themselves purchased the annex just six years earlier for only $75,000. Winfield sold his business interest in January 1910 for $350,000, making a $100,000 profit in less than two years.

The "old" Hotel Worth was destroyed by fire on February 3, 1945. (Courtesy UTA.)

Two

Growth of the City and Heyday of the Cattle Barons 1900–1920

The first two decades of the new century marked a period of tremendous growth in the lodging industry but also setbacks for the city and the country. Just after the fin de siècle, voices called for more hotel space and lamented that what was missing was a first-class luxury establishment. In 1901, the city had good hotels but no grand hotel, no hotel that could be called the greatest in Texas or the South. In November 1903, Capt. B.B. Paddock took the lead in making the city a "hotel center." He suggested to city leaders that a new hotel was necessary and that, in his opinion, the city was growing too fast not to have more luxury hotels.

Room shortages occurred each year during the Fat Stock Show. Hotels reported that all rooms were taken, some occupied by six to seven guests, while many travelers had to be turned away and sent to Dallas. In 1904, Paddock repeated his plea for a large hotel. He traveled to Chicago and St. Louis to talk with potential investors. The hotel he had in mind would feature at least 300 rooms and would cost about $250,000. While in the Midwest, Paddock also tried to drum up general business for the city, traveling with 10,000 pamphlets promoting Fort Worth. His plea was heard, for in 1910, the St. Louis brewery millionaire August Busch contemplated building a luxury hotel in Fort Worth, but only if the city would be able to raise $200,000 in stock. For that purpose, Busch purchased a city lot on Throckmorton Street between Third and Fourth Streets. In the end, though, he opted to build in Dallas.

Yet by 1909, business slowed, and there was an overabundance of smaller houses available. Many had not kept up with new technology and offered no amenities like hot running water or private baths. The city itself recuperated from the great flood of 1908. The city was still segregated, and the Main Hotel on Commerce Street across from the Majestic Theater and some smaller boardinghouses now served African American travelers.

Finally, by 1907, plans for a "grande" hotel were drawn up, and in 1910, the 300-room Westbrook Hotel opened. It was the first large lodging establishment of the new century. Fort Worth felt the effects of World War I almost immediately. While some business slowed, the building of the training grounds at Camp Bowie brought both new challenges and commerce to the city.

This turn-of-the-century photograph shows Winfield Scott (center), the owner of many hotels, standing next to his friend and business partner E.B. Harrold (right) and an unidentified man. Scott's hotel properties stretched from the foot of Main Street all the way to the courthouse, and by 1906, he received the highest tax bill in town. His future plans included a truly luxurious and elegant hotel named after him. Unfortunately, Scott passed away in October 1911 before his plans materialized. (Courtesy UTA.)

One of Winfield Scott's investment properties, the Terminal Hotel, was built in 1907 opposite Union Station on 1616 Main Street. The hotel was a four-story, 100-room property. Half of the rooms had private baths. Two older structures had been razed in order to make room for the Terminal. By October 1910, the hotel management was sold to a private investor, J.E. Hutt of Kansas City. In 1920, the hotel company of Sonderman, Powers, and Conrad Hilton leased the hotel and refurbished it for $160,000. The same group also operated the Melba Hotel. Before the Terminal was torn down, it operated as the Rail Hotel. (Courtesy Fort Worth City Directory.)

The 50-room Inman Hotel was built in 1908 by Winfield Scott but leased to Emma Inman. In 1911, the Inman was renamed the Scott Hotel and, eventually, the Plaza Hotel. The Scott, located at 303 Main Street, was one of Winfield Scott's smaller properties. It was a typical cattle-era hotel, built before the oil boom and large hotels. The oil boom in Texas brought an unexpected demand in office space, and in 1918, this hotel was converted into offices. In 1921, it reverted back to a hotel. The property was completely restored in 1981 and sits in what is now the heart of the city, close to Sundance Square. The photograph below shows an example of the green-and-white, glazed ornamental tiles on the three-story building. (Both, author's photograph.)

These photographs show the resting place of Winfield Scott, who was at one point the richest man in Fort Worth. Scott, one of the heaviest investors in property in the city, sold and purchased real estate, often at once. Properties on Main Street sold for as much as $1,200 a foot.

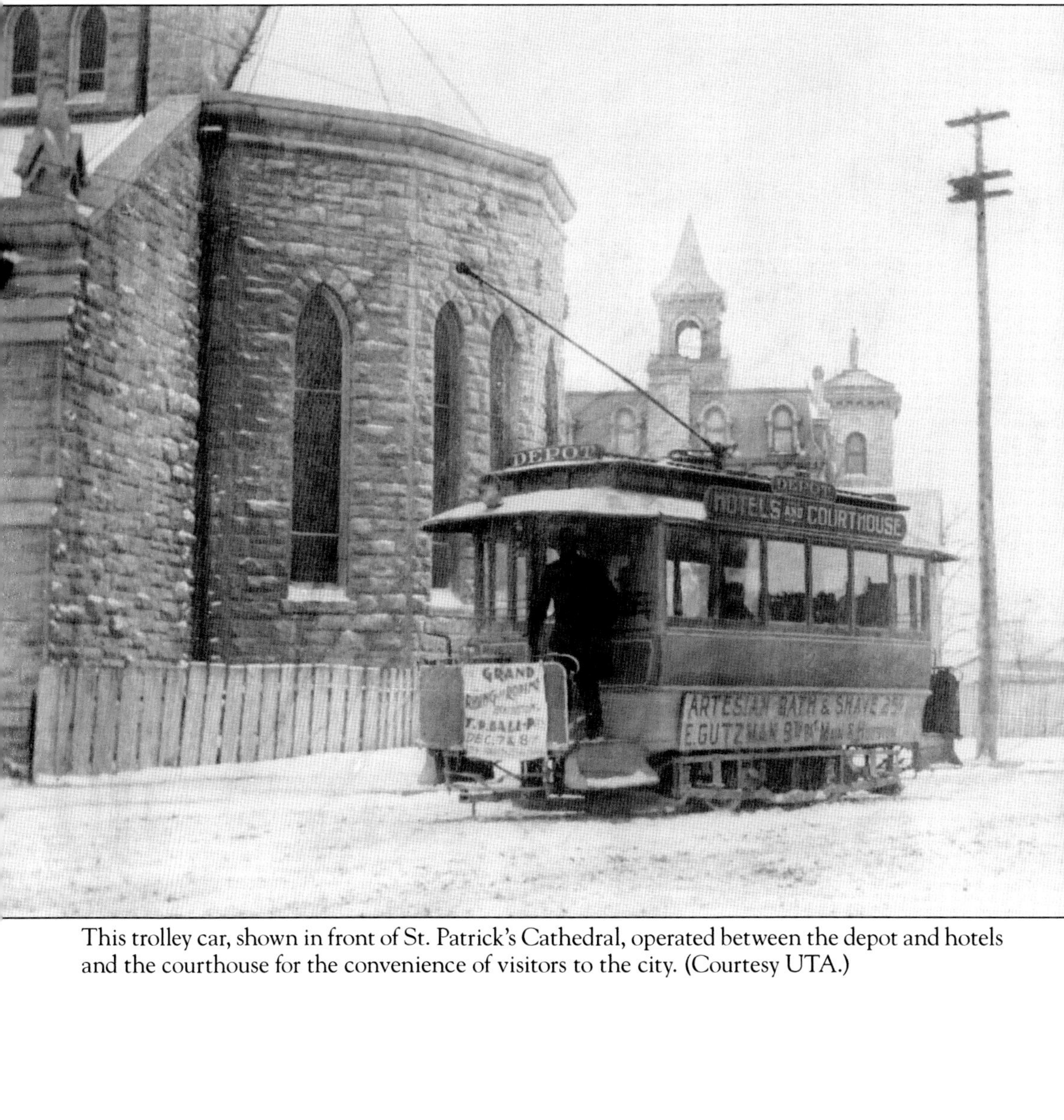

This trolley car, shown in front of St. Patrick's Cathedral, operated between the depot and hotels and the courthouse for the convenience of visitors to the city. (Courtesy UTA.)

Although technically not a hotel, the Stock Yards Club, originally located in Niles City, now North Fort Worth, was built by T.M. Thannisch in February 1904. The two-story wood frame structure had a large wraparound balcony, a billiard parlor, and a saloon. Furnished rooms were located on the second floor. The club opened in March 1904 and also housed an insurance firm, a restaurant, a barbershop, and a fruit and confectionery stand. (Courtesy North Fort Worth Historical Society.)

The three-story Stockyard Hotel was built by Col. Thomas Thannisch in 1906–1907 and enlarged in 1913 to its current size. The building was the first structure on Exchange Avenue in North Fort Worth. It was completed by March 1907 and had a restaurant, bar, and doctor's office. By 1913, the hotel was enlarged, matching the existing brickwork, and renamed Hotel Chandler. Originally comprising 86 rooms, some with baths, and with two community baths for the guests, the hotel after extensive renovations currently has 52 rooms. The Stockyard Hotel is located at the intersection of North Main Street and Exchange Avenue. It was built of cast stone and red brick and finished with geometrical decor. In 1933, the notorious gangster duo Bonnie Parker and Clyde Barrow rented a room on the third floor and hid from the authorities for almost a week. (Both, author's photograph.)

The above photograph shows the lobby of the Hotel Chandler in 1917. Behind the counter is R.L. Chandler, ready to serve her guests. The Chandler operated under this name until 1923 and prided itself on serving the wives and daughters of cattle ranchers. (Courtesy UTA.)

In 1924, the hotel was renamed Planters Hotel and operated under the management of J.W. Mott, who had purchased the hotel for $35,000. The hotel was later renamed Stockyard Hotel and, finally, the Right Hotel in 1950. The hotel is seen here in the 1970s. The fire escapes were added in the 1920s. In 1982, following extensive renovation, the building was renamed Stockyard Hotel yet again. (Courtesy North Fort Worth Historical Society.)

These photographs of the main lobby of the Stockyard Hotel include some of the original 1913 furnishings. (Both, author's photograph.)

The Hotel Court was a three-story brick building on 113 East Sixth Street at Commerce Street. According to the advertisement in the Forth Worth City Directory, the hotel prided itself on having the best liquor in town. The Hotel Court suffered major damage in 1954 during a water-heater explosion and was eventually demolished. (Courtesy Fort Worth Public Library.)

This building, located at 101 Houston Street, was built on the site that housed the first bank in Fort Worth, which was established in 1872 by Tidball & Wilson. The ground floor of the three-story brick building was used as a storefront, while the two upper floors housed the Hotel Green and later the Park Hotel. (Both, author's photograph.)

The Seibold Hotel, on the corner of Seventh and Rusk Streets, was hailed in March 1907 as a new four-story addition to the city's hotel ranks. The building was erected as the Tarrant County Courthouse. By 1898, the medical college occupied the location. The building was renovated, two stories were added, and the hotel was named after Edward Seibold, who financed the reconstruction. The Seibold Hotel was the first in the city to feature hot and cold water and telephones in every guest room. Edward Seibold became one of the first Oldsmobile owners in the city when he purchased a car from the Vernon Motor Car Company. The lobby was finished in marble-and-gold leaf onyx and mahogany furniture. Tiffany-style glass completed the decor. The hotel offered a "celebrated Sealy mattresses in every room." Later, a separate waiting room for ladies was installed on the second floor. In February 1913, the hotel received fire damage amounting to about $40,000 when the elevator caught fire and water soaked the rest of the building. One of the city's first Chinese restaurants operated in the Seibold. Although the hotel stayed in the Seibold family, Edward Seibold was involved in various court procedures as well as a bizarre incident in November 1918 when his throat was cut at his private residence. (Above, Fort Worth City Directory; below, courtesy FTWPL vertical file.)

SEIBOLD HOTEL COMPANY

MRS. DELLA WHEELER, President and Managing Director

SEVENTH AND COMMERCE STS. **Phone Lamar 3610**

FORT WORTH, TEXAS

The Touraine Hotel, located at the southwest corner of Seventh and Throckmorton Streets, opened on April 1, 1906. It was owned by W.W. Sloan Jr., who spared no expense on this three-story, European-style hotel. Mr. Miller, a well-known hotel and café man, was the proprietor. The executive chef, Mr. Van Hacken, had worked at the Baltimore Hotel in Kansas City. The hotel had 35 rooms, ranging in rates from $2 a day and up. The café could accommodate 125 guests and served lunch for 25¢. The Touraine featured Japanese-gilt paper and a jeweled glass ceiling. Although it was an instant hit with Fort Worth society and was used for a variety of banquets and gatherings, the hotel experienced financial difficulties shortly after opening and by 1908 had its third manager. It was eventually sold in June 1909 for $132,750 and converted into office suites and renamed the Chemical Building. By 1929, the architectural firm of Hedrick announced plans to demolish the old Touraine Hotel and to construct, at a cost of $1.5 million, an 18-story office building. (Author's postcard.)

These photographs show the Melba Hotel on Houston Street in 1920s (above) and c. 1907 (below). The Melba, located at 1107 Houston Street, was managed in 1907 by Simeon Naylor and in 1909 by W.E. Lestor. By May 1915, Ed Bush, who had been the chief clerk at the Metropolitan for 15 years, became the new part-owner of the Melba. (Both, author's postcards.)

Pictured above is an advertisement for the Melba Hotel.

The Elk's European Hotel, seen here on the right, was a two-story structure on Houston and Tenth Streets. It was operated by Kindle C. Maddox, who renamed it the Maddox European Hotel in 1909. By 1911, it was managed by Mabel Johnson. (Author's postcard.)

The former Star Hotel (renamed Manor Hotel), a turn-of-the-century structure, currently operates under the name Miss Molly's Hotel at 200 West Exchange Avenue in the Fort Worth Stockyards. It was built in 1910, but it did not become a hotel until 1930. It offers eight rooms. W.W. Seibel ran a boardinghouse in this two-story brick structure for the growing number of packing plant workers. From the mid-1920s on, the building was rented by Louis Brown, who operated one of his three boardinghouses on the second floor.

This three-story brick structure, located in the historic Stockyards district, was erected around 1915. The Magnolia Furniture Company occupied the bottom floor, while one of the three Brown's Boarding Houses was located on the upper floors. The words "Board and Rooms" can still be seen on the side of the building (below). The boardinghouse was then converted into a hotel and renamed Stockman's Hotel. (Both, author's photograph.)

The brick structure seen in the foreground of the photograph at left was erected in 1919 at the southwest corner of Calhoun and Eighth Streets to serve as a garage and livery service for the planned Winfield Hotel (renamed Hotel Texas). The garage had a capacity of 325 cars and included a car elevator and wash racks. The Hotel Texas can be seen in the background in the photograph at left. In the photograph below can be seen the back of the garage. In 1920, Fort Worth's first automobile show was held at the Winfield garage with almost 70 cars and trucks participating. It still bears Winfield Scott's name. (Both, author's photograph.)

By April 1907, plans were made public about a new 10-story hotel that would replace the Delaware Hotel. The goal was to construct an up-to-date, fireproof, 300-room building. The management of the Delaware stipulated, however, that if Tarrant County became a dry county, the contemplated hotel would not be built as planned. In the end, plans were scaled back, and the Westbrook ended up being a seven-story building. Ben Tillar paid $65,000 in November 1908 for the site, later adding the adjacent property, worth $100,000, in order to build the hotel. The Westbrook officially opened on December 15, 1910, with a telegraph system and steel towers on its roof and its own artisan wells. The hotel was a reinforced concrete building nicknamed the "Oil Lease Center of the World." (Author's postcard.)

A military parade in 1917 passes in front of the Westbrook Hotel, adjacent to the Dexter Hotel. (Courtesy General Photograph Collection, UTSA Libraries Special Collections, Institute of Texan Cultures.)

The Westbrook is seen here on a 1940s postcard sold by the hotel. Note the added fire escape on the far left side of the building and the added marquees. A. Magnuson became the Westbrook's new manager in February 1921. He had been previously employed in St. Louis property. (Author's postcard.)

These photographs show a vintage hotel key and leather tags from the Westbrook (above) and a souvenir silver spoon (below). Both items are now located in the Tarrant County Archives. (Both, photograph by author; courtesy TCA.)

To set itself apart, the Westbrook offered Japanese tea ceremonies to its guests. The hotel featured 302 rooms, all with private toilets, and 200 rooms had baths with hot and cold water and telephone access. For the convenience of the guests, two elevators were available. The ballroom, located on the top floor, could accommodate 500 guests and, after a renovation, was able to fit 2,000 guests. The Westbrook cost $1 million to build, and it was decorated with imported green Italian and Swiss marble and golden accents. No electric lighting was needed during the day because of the layout and construction of the airy lobby and rooms.

With the widespread use of the automobile, a new headache for hoteliers of older properties arrived. Many did not have the space to offer parking, especially those located downtown. By the time Elvis Presley stayed in room 568 on April 20, 1956, the Westbrook charged $4 a night. (Author's postcard.)

The lobby of the Westbrook is seen here shortly before the building's demolition. The last remnants of the hotel, in this case, mattresses, were being removed.

The beloved "Golden Goddess" was a symbol of good luck and prosperity among Texas oilmen of the 1920s. It is seen here around 1974 in the lobby of the Westbrook Hotel. The Goddess is currently located in the Fort Worth Petroleum Club. (Courtesy Tarrant County Archives and UTA.)

By the mid-1930s, the Westbrook had declined, and it finally closed in 1969. A year later, it opened as a retirement home, but then shut its doors for good in 1973. An obscure discovery took place when the former hotel was being prepared for demolition. Workers located a 45-year-old urn that had been placed in storage when the owner moved to Washington, DC. In January 1978, what had once been the best-known hotel in the region was imploded. (Both, courtesy UTA.)

Three

Oil Boom and Great Depression 1920–1940

The oil boom in Texas replaced the old cattle barons with throngs of adventurers and a flood of new money. In 1919, a decade after Winfield Scott's death, voices in the city became loud again to finally build the luxury hotel he had once envisioned. In January 1921, a total of $300,000 in stock was raised to move forward. It had become clear that private individuals alone were not able to build hotels of this magnitude anymore. Therefore, a hotel company, headed by William Monnig, was created. But this opened the door for a national or even international company; the hotel would no longer be managed by locals. All citizens were encouraged to invest; Ed Farmer provided $17,000, and W.C. Stripling followed with a $9,000 investment. The decision to build the hotel was a wise one for the city of Fort Worth as well. The chamber of commerce estimated that in 1921, the city earned $5 million through conventions alone.

The Baker Company of San Antonio was entrusted to run the planned establishment and named it after Scott. Nevertheless, just before opening, Baker opted for a more generic name, the Hotel Texas. It officially opened on December 3, 1921, and over 1,000 guests from all over the nation were invited. The Texas had the largest banquet facility in the South and could accommodate 1,400 diners. With the arrival of the Texas, older hotels now found themselves scrambling for business.

Major facilities and other businesses arrived in Fort Worth during that time as well. In 1927, Meecham Field, the city's first municipal airport, opened, and in 1931, a new Texas & Pacific Rail terminal was built. Out of the need for new beds, in 1929, a new lodging structure was erected at Fifth and Main Streets. The hotel was named the Bluebonnet Hotel but would eventually be called the Blackstone Hotel and be managed by the Wallace N. Robinson Hotel Company. The 22-story Blackstone cost $1 million to build and $500,000 to furnish. The official opening in October 1929 was considered one of the major social events of the year in the city.

Smaller lodging places were built, but, during this time, some of the older hotels in Fort Worth were devastated by fire. In December 1920, the Mansion was ruined by fire, as was the Grammer Hotel. In 1928, the Ellison Hotel burned down.

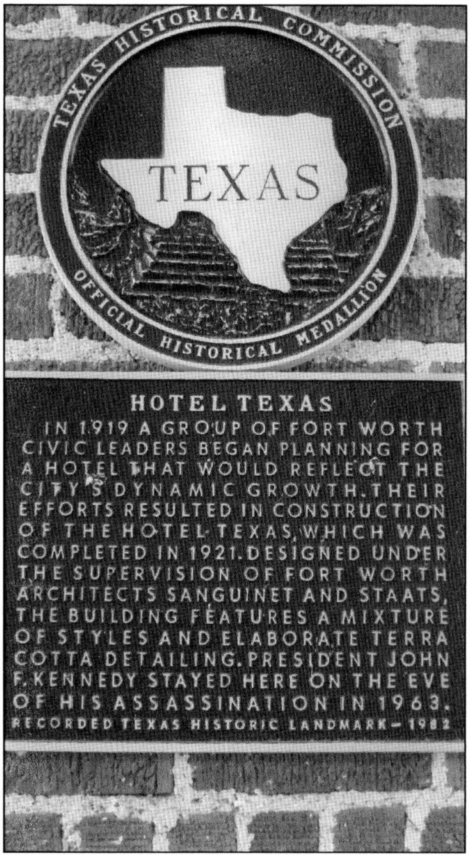

In 1919, a coalition of 27 leading citizens, including Amon Carter, W.C. Stripling, and William Monnig, saw the need for a new luxury hotel, and they formed the Citizens Hotel Committee. The Hotel Texas (below) was built next to the original Hotel Worth in an English Georgian style with terra-cotta ornamented brick. The lobby was a block long running from Main to Commerce Streets. The Texas had 600 rooms, three kitchens, and was 14 stories high. The hotel opened with lots of fanfare, and hotel men from all over the nation came for the opening celebrations. The Hotel Texas was hailed as the South's most splendid hostelry and a magnificent hotel. (Left, courtesy Tarrant County archives; below, author's postcard.)

One of the first guests at the newly opened Texas was Puerto Rico governor E. Mont Reily in December 1921. The hotel was comparable to any good hotel in the East. To stay as authentic to Texan roots as possible, the names of the ballrooms and banquet halls were Blue Bonnet, Cactus Room, The Blue Bonnet Promenade, Hall of Longhorns, and South Room. The china was purchased locally from Gernsbacher Brothers on Houston Street. The American-made china cost $15,000; the banquet china, decorated in black and gold, cost $1,500; and the glassware used in the hotel cost $3,500. Edwin Lee was named general manager of the new establishment. Room rates were $2 and up. The Texas was the first hotel of its size and importance in the country that returned to the prewar rate of $2 for a room and bath.

The 1920s postcard (above) depicts the Hotel Texas's Keystone Room. The photograph below shows the same ballroom after an extensive renovation in the summer of 1950. (Above, author's postcard; below, courtesy UTA.)

The Texas landed a major business deal before it even opened in 1920, when the Cattle Raisers' Association of Texas made it their official headquarters hotel. Throughout its years of operation, the hotel was able to book major conventions, like the Hereford Association in 1940, the American Legion in 1944, and the Kiwanis in 1948. In this 1935 advertisement, the Texas describes itself as the city's largest and most popular hotel. The hotel offered a new service to commercial travelers by eliminating the day rate. This was geared particularly to patrons who only stayed in Fort Worth for a few hours on business and needed a place to freshen up without having to pay for a full day's charge. The Texas prided itself on attention to detail and in making a stay as pleasant as possible. Colgate's finest soap, the "Cashmere Bouquet," could be found in the guest bathrooms.

In 1936, the Baker Hotel Company no longer managed the Hotel Texas; it was now managed by the Citizens Hotel Company of Fort Worth. The company spent $200,000 to redecorate and refurbish the hotel in anticipation of the city's centennial celebration. This photograph shows Main Street in the late 1940s with the Milner Hotel on the far right and the Texas at right on the next block. (Author's postcard.)

World War I veterans participating in the Armistice Day Parade pass in front of the Hotel Texas on November 11, 1941, a few weeks before US entrance into World War II. (Courtesy UTA.)

Pres. John F. Kennedy is seen here on the morning of November 22, 1963, leaving the Hotel Texas, where he spent his last night in suite 805. Texas governor John Connally booked 150 rooms in early November for the visit. A nonpartisan breakfast, which included Vice Pres. Lyndon Johnson, was set up in the grand ballroom on that fateful day in November. (Courtesy UTA.)

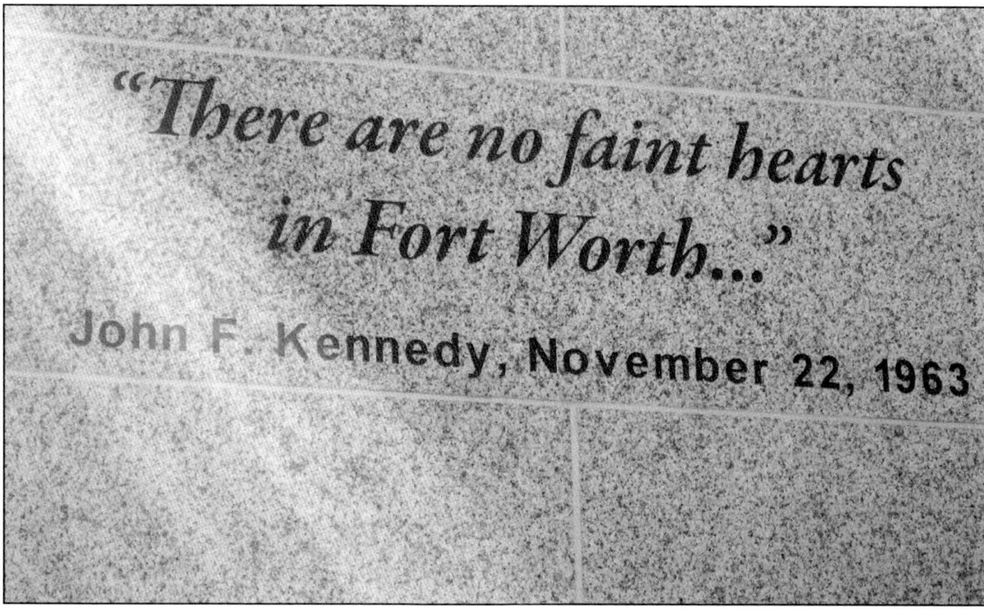

In November 2012, the City of Fort Worth opened the John F. Kennedy Memorial, commemorating the president's last speech, delivered at the adjacent former Hotel Texas, which operates currently as a Hilton property. (Both, author's photograph.)

Among the detailed masonry on the Hotel Texas are symbols resembling cow skulls. (Both, author's photograph.)

In this marquee sign, the Hotel Texas advertises the city of Fort Worth, "Where the West Begins." (Courtesy UTA.)

This photograph shows the grand ballroom in the convention center. The room seated up to 3,000 people for a meeting and up to 2,000 for dining. The room could be further subdivided into three smaller rooms. The Hotel Texas was managed in the 1960s by the Sheraton company, which signed a 20-year lease. By then, plans were made public for a new 380-room hotel and transportation center to be built adjacent to the Texas. The hotel, however, never materialized. In October 1967, the Hotel Texas became the property of the Fort Worth Chamber of Commerce, which announced a $6.2-million face-lift, including a 230-room annex, pool, and parking garage. (Author's postcard.)

Shown here is the Llano Hotel on Twenty-fourth Street and Ellis Avenue near the historic Stockyards in North Fort Worth. The three-story brick building, constructed in 1924, had 58 rooms and was later named the Frontier Hotel. In 1978, the hotel was condemned and closed for good. The three-story structure in the background is the Stockman Hotel. The Llano building is listed in the National Register of Historic Places. (Courtesy North Fort Worth Historical Society.)

The Alps Hotel is seen here in the 1930s. The brick hotel was erected in 1910 and originally operated as the Ashby & Dill Grocery. The second floor then became Sally Smith's Boarding House and finally the Alps Hotel. The building, located at 222 West Exchange Avenue, was restored in 1983 and is now listed in the National Register of Historic Places. (Courtesy North Fort Worth Historical Society.)

This is the Hotel Anne and Café, located in the Stockyards on Twenty-eighth Street. (Courtesy North Fort Worth Historical Society.)

This photograph shows the construction of the Elks Club and Hotel, which was built in 1928 at West Fourth and Burnet Streets. Although no longer used as a hotel, the building still stands; it once served as the downtown YMCA. (Courtesy John Avila, Thos. S. Byrne Construction.)

The old Elk's Club and downtown YMCA building, seen here in a current photograph, was constructed in a Georgian Revival style. (Author's photograph.)

This 1920s photograph shows the Hotel Diana and Hotel Dean on lower Main Street. This section of town was previously known as Hell's Half Acre. These and several other hotels, like the Majestic Hotel, the Madoc Hotel, and Trinity Hotel, were demolished to make way for the Tarrant County Convention Center. (Courtesy UTA.)

After the opening of the Texas, older facilities, once considered elegant houses, had a hard time attracting business. Therefore, by the mid-1920s, a "new" Worth Hotel was planned. The 18-story building at Seventh and Taylor Streets opened in September 1927. The Hotel Worth had 300 rooms, each with its own bath and all the latest amenities, including ceiling fans. The hotel also had a café shop, a ballroom, a barbershop for the male guests, and a beauty parlor for the ladies. (Courtesy UTA.)

The above photograph was taken during a parade for the premier of the movie *The Westerner* in September 1940. Passing in front of the Worth Hotel, on the white horse, is Gary Cooper. Riding next to Cooper is Amon Carter, waving to the crowd of enthusiastic fans. The photograph below shows the entrance of the Hotel Worth. (Both, courtesy UTA.)

The photograph at right documents the end of an era. The Hotel Worth is imploded as onlookers watch on October 29, 1972. Below, Willie White, who had been with the Hotel Worth as a room service waiter since 1936, is seen leaving the hotel for the last time in February 1972. (Both, courtesy UTA.)

The Blackstone Hotel opened on October 23, 1929. Construction costs for the hotel, which at the time was the tallest reinforced steel building in the United States, totaled $800,000. Later, a banquet hall was added on the second floor of the hotel for $40,000. The 23-story tan bricked Gothic Revival and Art Deco–inspired hotel originally had 250 rooms, a Venetian ballroom, and, by 1952, the first rooftop outdoor swimming pool in the city. The photograph below shows the outdoor courtyard on the 16th floor of the Blackstone Hotel. (Left, courtesy Tarrant County Archives; below, courtesy UTA.)

Above, the entrance of the Blackstone Hotel on Main Street is seen in 1949. The Hilton Hotel Company managed the Blackstone from 1952 to 1962 and spent close to $2 million in major renovations and updates. The photograph below shows the redecorated lobby in November 1954. (Both, courtesy UTA.)

Over the years, the hotel has hosted its share of politicians and celebrities. Herbert Hoover, Franklin Roosevelt, Richard Nixon, and Lyndon B. Johnson stayed at the Blackstone, as did Clark Cable, Gene Autry, Frank Sinatra, and Benny Goodman, among many others. In August 1962, the hotel was purchased by Richard D. Walker, who planned to convert it into a luxury apartment hotel. The plans never materialized, and in 1964, it was sold at auction in only 17 minutes for half a million dollars. The following year, the hotel was in trouble again, and the 20 permanent guests were told to vacate by September. The hotel briefly lost its name in November 1965, when it operated as the Golden West Hotel. After that, it sat empty until 1968, when $2 million was spent on a face-lift, which included a 330-car parking garage. (Author's postcard.)

By October 1982, the Blackstone was bankrupt. It closed its doors and sat empty until 1999. It now operates under the Marriott Corporation as a Courtyard with 203 guest rooms. The photograph at right shows the hotel's detailed terra-cotta ornamental masonry work. The hotel was built on the site of the former Rialto Theater and cattle rancher millionaire Christopher O'Keefe envisioned a hotel for him and his fellow ranchers to hang out while conducting business in the city. Unfortunately, O'Keefe died just three months after the Blackstone received its first guest. Thc photograph below shows a guest draft from the Blackstone. (Right, author's photograph; below, courtesy Tarrant County Archives.)

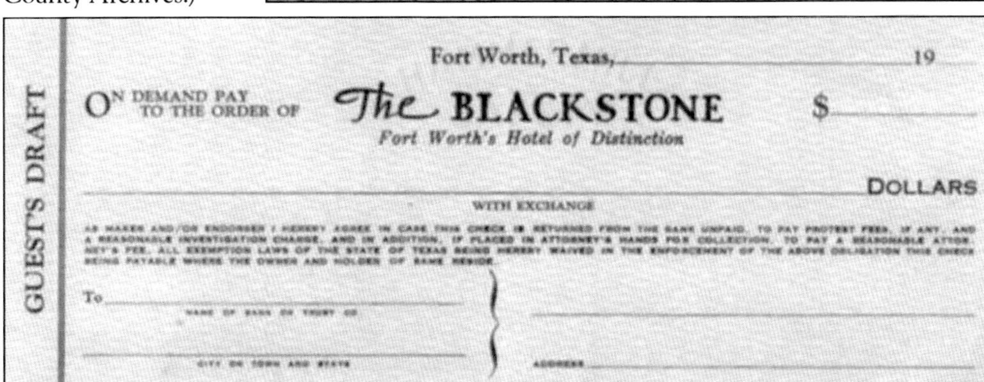
GUEST'S DRAFT

Fort Worth, Texas,____________ 19___

ON DEMAND PAY TO THE ORDER OF The BLACKSTONE $______

Fort Worth's Hotel of Distinction

____________ DOLLARS

WITH EXCHANGE

AS MAKER AND/OR ENDORSER I HEREBY AGREE IN CASE THIS CHECK IS RETURNED FROM THE BANK UNPAID, TO PAY PROTEST FEES, IF ANY, AND A REASONABLE INVESTIGATION CHARGE, AND IN ADDITION, IF PLACED IN ATTORNEY'S HANDS FOR COLLECTION, TO PAY A REASONABLE ATTORNEY'S FEE. ALL EXEMPTION LAWS OF THE STATE OF TEXAS BEING HEREBY WAIVED IN THE ENFORCEMENT OF THE ABOVE OBLIGATION THIS CHECK BEING PAYABLE WHERE THE OWNER AND HOLDER OF SAME RESIDE.

To____________
NAME OF BANK OR TRUST CO

____
CITY OR TOWN AND STATE

ADDRESS____________

In 1936, the Blackstone advertised dancing with Richard Cole and his orchestra for an entrance fee of $1.65 per couple. Room service in 1947 was offered between 5:30 p.m. and 9:30 p.m., hardly the 24-hour service expected today from a first-class hotel. That year, a fresh salmon steak with anchovy butter cost a guest $1.60, and a bottle of either Schlitz or Muehlebach beer was 30¢. A peach shortcake cost 40¢, and a coffee was 20¢. (Courtesy Tarrant County Archives.)

Shown here is the Victor Hotel shortly before demolition to make way for the Tarrant County Convention Center on lower Main Street. (Courtesy UTA.)

The 35-room Victorian Inn was built in 1922 at the corner of Hemphill Street and Jefferson Avenue in a Mission, Colonial Revival style. The building eventually reached such a state of dilapidation that it was forced to close in 2007. The empty structure burned in January 2012 and was eventually torn down. (Both, courtesy David A. Matthews.)

In August 1936, the El Patio Lodge Incorporation raised $1,000 in stock and started plans to build a tourist lodge. Ready for the summer season of 1938, the El Patio Lodge opened in June of that year to the public. The hotel, hailed as the only air-conditioned tourist lodge, was located at East Lancaster Avenue and Highway 80. The El Patio was a white stucco structure with orange awnings and blue shutters. It featured hot and cold showers and a grillroom serving chicken and steak dinners. (Author's postcard.)

The Hotel Texas, located in the historic Stockyards on Ellis Avenue, is not to be confused with the original Hotel Texas downtown. The 21-room Hotel Texas, shown in the above photograph, was built in 1939 and featured a yellow tile brick exterior. It formerly operated under the name Exchange Hotel. As another example of the shift from downtown lodging facilities to motor hotels located on highways, the Fort Worth Tourist Motel (below) featured 24-hour service and was equipped with kitchenettes for the traveling public. (Above, author's photograph; below, courtesy FTWPL.)

The Trav'O'Tel Shady Tour Rest Motel, shown above, was located on East Belknap. The photograph below depicts the Westmore Courts on Camp Bowie. In 1958, the Westmore was able to charge $6.50 for a single room and $7.50 for double occupancy. (Above, author's postcard; below, courtesy TCA.)

This photo postcard of the Rockaway Court offers another example of a motor hotel located on Camp Bowie. (Courtesy TCA.)

Another photo postcard shows the Westmoor Court. This motor hotel featured a gas station and club. (Courtesy TCA.)

Four

War and the Rise of the Automobile 1940–1960

New challenges for hotel operators in the early 1940s did not come in the form of guest demands, but rather in terms of safety and security for the guest. The first blackout decrees were implemented in January 1942 because of the fear of air raids from secret fields in Mexico, and the Texas Hotel Association saw it necessary to release uniform blackout procedures for all hotels. Guest speakers and conventions centered on the war and the war effort. The chamber of commerce's yearly dinner in 1942 at the Hotel Texas included a "war theme." But the ever-growing defense industry also brought business into the city. In 1941, in Fort Worth alone, 360 companies received defense contracts totaling $45 million. The Consolidated Aircraft Corporation broke ground on a bomber plant on the west side of the city. After the war, Fort Worth became the second largest aircraft production center in America, and in the late 1950s, the region had the most active oil wells in the world. Travelers now demanded air-conditioned facilities, ice makers, and pools.

The general shift in the US lodging industry that had started at the beginning of the war also affected Fort Worth. Fewer big city hotels were built, while the number of motels and motor courts in the United States mushroomed, from about 13,000 in 1939 to more than 30,000 in 1950. The first motels appeared in the 1920s with the development of the highway system, and the concept peaked in the 1950s and 1960s, particularly with the ending of wartime gas rationing. Further stimulating the building of motor lodges and motels was the introduction of five major highways across the city. By 1940, the US motel industry had annual revenues of $37 million but also a bad reputation. FBI chief J. Edgar Hoover believed that "the tourist motels were a new home of crime in America, a new home of disease, bribery, corruption, crookedness, rape, white slavery, thievery, and murder." This trend was also evident in Fort Worth.

After the war, the city's population grew, reaching 278,778 in 1950. The oil and aeronautical industries dominated the economy in the city. Fort Worth was better off than other Texas cities; it was still able to attract large annual conventions and visitors. In 1951, Bell Helicopter moved its plant to Fort Worth, further adding to the need of hotel and meeting space and long-term accommodations. Out of that need came the concept of a combined hotel and apartment facility.

Shown in the above postcard is the Colonial Hotel at Camp Bowie, an early example of a hotel combined with a long-term lodging facility. The two-story, imposing facility was built in 1942. It was one of the first places in Fort Worth that offered pizza. During its early days, the Colonial served refreshments in an enclosed tea garden. Later, however, the establishment's business dwindled and only attracted long-term boarders and prostitutes. It was eventually torn down. The Motor Inn Hotel (below), located on Camp Bowie Boulevard, claimed to be Fort Worth's finest suburban hotel. It offered air-conditioned rooms and tiled baths. (Both, author's postcard.)

Shown here are two early examples of motor lodges on Highway 80. These simple structures were often built in a "circle the wagon" layout. The hotels offered few amenities. These photographs of the Mission Courts (above) and the Trav-O-Tel (below) are both from 1942. (Both, courtesy Library of Congress, Prints & Photographs Division.)

The Loring Hotel was located on the six-point intersection of University Drive and Camp Bowie. It opened in 1949 and featured 105 rooms in a two-story, semi–Art Deco, U-shaped building. The hotel catered to performers from the Casa Manana. For the convenience of the guests, it had air-conditioning, tub and shower facilities, radio and television, ample parking, and a pool (above). Every morning, the *Fort Worth Star Telegram* was available to guests. By the mid-1950s, the Loring Hotel was owned by Leo Corrigan, a Dallas real estate and hotel executive. However, the facility fell into disrepair and was later used as a retirement hotel. It was torn down by the early 1990s to make room for new developments. (Above, author's postcard; below, photograph by Cindy Yamanaka, *Dallas Morning News*.)

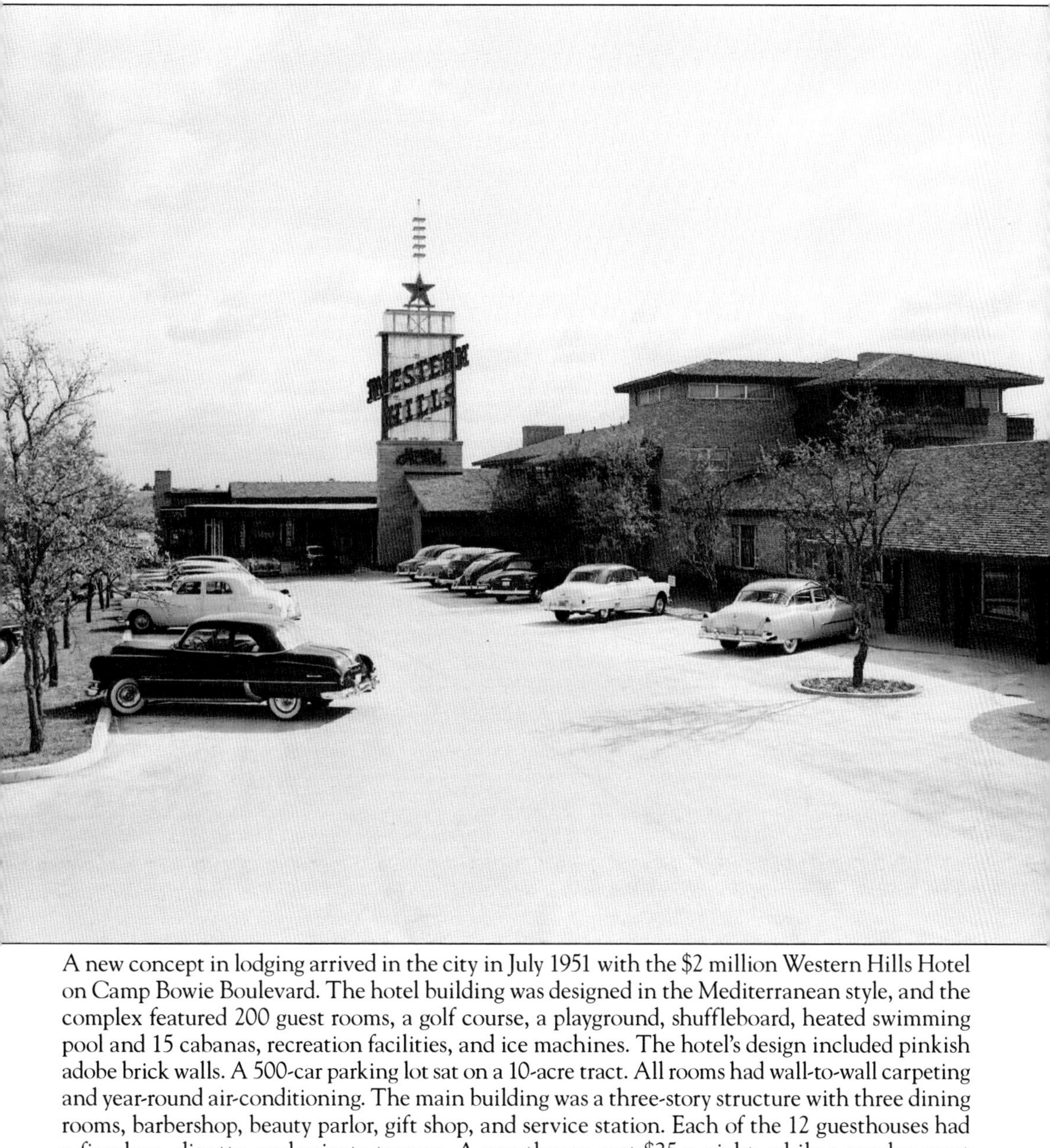

A new concept in lodging arrived in the city in July 1951 with the $2 million Western Hills Hotel on Camp Bowie Boulevard. The hotel building was designed in the Mediterranean style, and the complex featured 200 guest rooms, a golf course, a playground, shuffleboard, heated swimming pool and 15 cabanas, recreation facilities, and ice machines. The hotel's design included pinkish adobe brick walls. A 500-car parking lot sat on a 10-acre tract. All rooms had wall-to-wall carpeting and year-round air-conditioning. The main building was a three-story structure with three dining rooms, barbershop, beauty parlor, gift shop, and service station. Each of the 12 guesthouses had a fireplace, dinette, and private terrace. A guesthouse cost $25 a night, while a regular guest room ranged from between $4 and $50. Hotel personnel stayed in available basement rooms on the property. Western Hills Hotel revolutionized the motor hotel industry in the United States. The resort-style hotel drew large crowds from neighboring cities, and many used the hotel for a "quickie vacation." (Courtesy UTA.)

GOOD LIVING AT ITS RE

Western Hills offers the ultimate in comfort anc designed for your pleasure. For your added enj *swimming pool* (heated for year-round use), nearby, *free shuffleboard* and many other *complir*

TWIN BEDROOM

DELUXE SUITE

B

DOUBLE BEDROOM

WESTERN HILLS ACCOMMODATIONS inclu hotel proper and in private guest houses, po rooms with double, twin or studio beds. No where the custom-designed furnishings are ide different. Providing luxury and comfort are full front sliding closet doors, burn and stain foam rubber cushioned beds and chairs, gl less light, radio, shower and tub in every room.

STUDIO BEDROOM

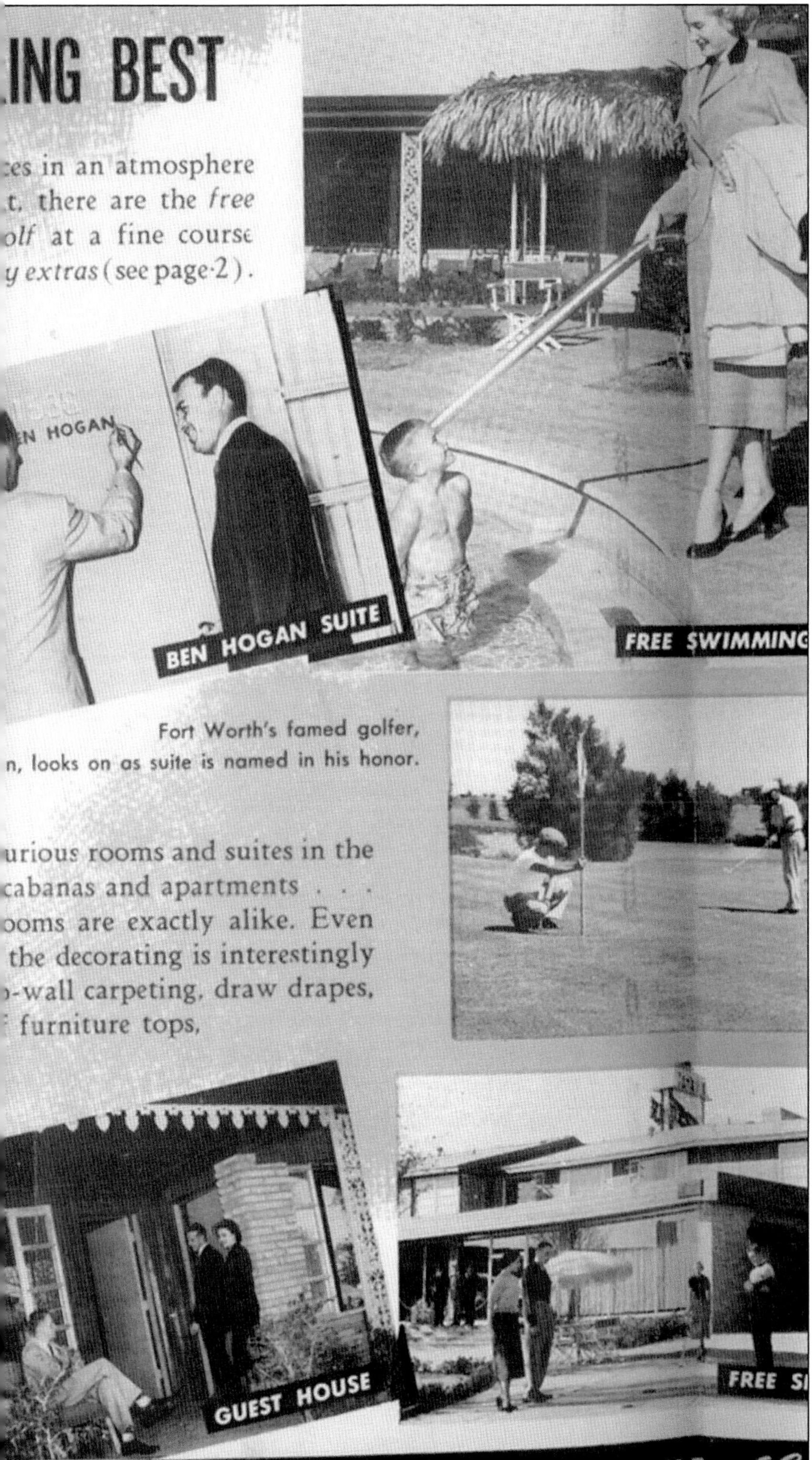

Shown here is a full-page advertisement for the Western Hills Hotel. (Courtesy Tarrant County Archives.)

The above photograph offers another view of the busy parking lot at the Western Hills. The world's first officially designated hotel heliport opened here in May 1953 with two Bell 47EM helicopters landing. Guests could now be shuffled to Carter Airfield in just 15 minutes. In the photograph below, from early 1952, guests enjoy themselves at the outdoor pool. (Both, author's postcard.)

The lobby of the Western Hills is seen here in 1951. The facility offered twin, double, studio, and deluxe suites in addition to private guesthouses and poolside cabanas. Hollywood celebrities who stayed in the Western Hills included Jerry Lewis, Bob Hope, Joan Crawford, and Lucille Ball and her husband, Desi Arnaz, who later opened a Western Hills in California, modeled after the one in Fort Worth. By July 1964, however, Western Hills was in debt. It closed and was auctioned off to the former owner, H.S. Green, for only $700,000. A two-alarm fire in April 1969 caused minor damage, but a four-alarm fire in September wrought massive damage. In July 1970, the Western Hills Hotel was torn down to make way for a shopping center. (Courtesy UTA.)

The Western Hills, Fort Worth's "Exciting Hotel," featured, after extensive renovation, a Polynesian Village. The South Sea was re-created by converting the cabanas into authentic tropical bamboo huts and using hundreds of turtle shells in the dining room.

The Fortune Arms Hotel was the first major downtown hotel built after the war. The 10-story red and tan brick structure cost $2.5 million in 1951. By 1959, however, the hotel was in financial difficulties and was sold in auction within minutes. The Fortune Arms featured a pool, retail shops, public dining, and parking spaces for 100 cars. It was eventually renamed Birkley Apartment Hotel, then Hunter Plaza, and is currently used as commercial space. (Right, author's photograph; below, artist rendering, *Dallas Morning News*.)

The Rio Hotel, located on 6600 Camp Bowie Boulevard, was built in 1959 as a motor hotel typical of the era. It featured a two-story structure with 125 rooms, a pool, and coffee shop. However, just five years after the grand opening, the hotel was involved in a legal battle with the Western Hills Hotel and was sold for $124,000 in August 1964. The furniture and other inventory, assessed separately, were valued at $26,000. The Landmark Lodge (below) was another example of a property that marketed itself to the traveling community. The Landmark Lodge was located at Highways 80 and 180. (Both, author's postcard.)

A 60-room, air-conditioned property known as the Century Motel was located on East Lancaster Avenue. All rooms featured private baths, radio, and television. The Century was a Duncan Hines–approved motel. The Duncan Hines company, now better known for its cake-mix products, published a lodging guide starting in the 1930s. The company would travel the country and recommend restaurants and hotels. (Both, author's postcard.)

The Desert Village Motel was another example of 1950s motels in Fort Worth. Since most motels were located outside the downtown area, coffee shops and other amenities were offered to the traveling public. A double room set a traveler back $8 a night in 1958. (Author's postcard.)

The Park Plaza Motel, with its eye-catching neon sign, offered a pool, television, and fine foods. The facility was approved by the American Automobile Association. (Author's postcard.)

Shown here are two more examples of motels during the golden era of motor lodges. The Drummers Inn and Continental Inn both featured outdoor pools, cafés, and ample guest parking. (Both, author's postcard.)

Five

Urban Decay and Renewal

1960 and Beyond

The trend of locating lodging facilities along the highway system continued until 1962, when the construction of a seven-story downtown Towers Hotel was announced. Urban renewal, a trend in most major cities, also took place in Fort Worth. Smaller, inefficient, and often dilapidated lodging sites were torn down. In 1965, the Reliance Hotel, once operated by the Salvation Army, made way for the parking lot of the Lone Star Gas Company; the Sally was condemned and eventually closed down; and the Westbrook was a victim of the wrecking ball in 1978. The Cowtown Inn, a three-story motel that had opened in 1964, closed in 1990 and sat empty for 15 years until it was finally torn down. As early as 1960, city leaders realized that in order to attract major conventions, a downtown auditorium with at least 5,000 seats was needed. Blocks of downtown Fort Worth were torn down to make room for the new convention center. In 1965, a new motor inn, across from the new center, opened with big fanfare as the first hostelry built downtown in 35 years.

The chamber of commerce had even bigger plans at that time, and a Chicago firm determined the need for an even larger downtown property. Several large hotels, like a 500-room, $31-million hotel planned as a Fort Worth Ramada Inn on county property east of the convention center, did not materialize. Later plans included a proposed hotel with a 415-foot observation tower wrapped in glass.

In 1974, the Dallas Fort Worth International Airport opened, and 1978 rang in an era of downtown renewal, beginning with the Tandy Center and Americana Hotel and the renovation of the Hotel Texas, which operated as a Hyatt Regency. In 1980, the metropolitan population of Fort Worth reached one million people. In the early 1990s, the city struggled again as a convention center city, since Fort Worth was not a tourist destination like Austin and had difficulties attracting corporate travelers. Today, however, Fort Worth, known for its hospitality, charms almost eight million visitors a year.

In the spring of 1960, test drills were conducted for a proposed 28-story, 600-room hotel complex with a combined convention center that could accommodate up to 6,500 guests. The proposed facility would be built on Tenth and Taylor Streets, east of Monroe Street, at an estimated cost of $25 million. The complex, however, did not materialize. (Courtesy UTA.)

The Forest Park Motor Hotel prided itself as an accommodation at modest prices in a beautiful forest park. The property offered comfortable rooms and executive suites, catering service for groups, a pool, bonded babysitters, and complimentary morning coffee. The property was located on South University Drive, within a block of Jimmie Dip's Chinese food and Smitty's Pancake House. A sister property, the Clayton Motel, was located in Denton, Texas. (Above, courtesy TCA; below, author's postcard.)

This artist rendering shows the Green Oaks Inn, located in the Ridgmar section of Fort Worth. The Green brothers, who successfully operated the Western Hills, announced plans in June 1964 to build the Green Oaks Inn & Conference Center. The inn had 282 rooms in five separate buildings, two pools, and a waterfall. Green Oaks was built in a Texas Tudor style—a mingling of an Old English village and southwest architecture. It was designed by David George, a one-time apprentice of Frank Lloyd Wright. (Both, author's postcard.)

The Green Oaks Inn was an instant success and counted Bob Hope, Elvis Presley, Ronald Reagan, and Tina Turner among its guests. It was marketed as the ideal suburban oasis, just minutes from General Dynamics and Carswell Air Force Base. The kitchen and catering department were run by the German duo of Hans Lauer and Hermann Jung. In January 1974, Green Oaks was sold to a Minnesota company, which refurbished the establishment in a more contemporary look. After 42 years in operation, the complex was torn down in 2007. (Author's postcard.)

The Downtowner Motor Inn opened in April 1965, the first new downtown hostelry in 35 years. It stood across from the convention center and next to the Flat Iron Building. The five-story, 124-room, L-shaped building had exterior walkways. Each room was distinctively decorated. The Downtowner featured television and hi-fi music in the rooms and a heated pool. The basement garage had spaces for 90 automobiles. In 1967, the hotel was involved in a trademark infringement lawsuit. (Courtesy UTA.)

The former Downtowner Motor Inn changed names, and its status changed from an independent hotel to part of a national chain in 1993, when Days Inn took over the property. Currently, the hotel operates as the Park Central Inn. A new fountain, featuring a panther (right), the symbol of the city of Fort Worth, was installed a few years ago in front of the hotel. (Both, author's photograph.)

The Rodeway Inn Motel was built in October 1961 on the outskirts of downtown, close to the freeway. It was located on Lancaster Avenue and Henderson Road. This view of the motel is looking north toward the downtown skyline. It had 175 rooms and suites on seven floors. Its underground parking garage could also be used as a fallout shelter. However, nine months into construction, the structure collapsed. A new building technique that used lift slaps was blamed for the mishap, which set completion of the motel back for months. (Courtesy Jack White Photograph Collection, Special Collections, UTA.)

Shown here are two views of the Holiday Inn located in the city. The hotel stood at Vicery Boulevard and University Drive and featured the Cooper Hearth dining room. What made the hotel chain so attractive was the fact that travelers could use their Gulf credit cards to charge food and lodging expenses. In return, Gulf built gas stations on many of Holiday Inn's properties. (Both, author's postcard.)

Here is another photograph of a Holiday Inn in Fort Worth. The hotel chain was established in part because Kemmons Wilson, its founder, was unable to find a quality and consistent hotel when he travelled. The first inns opened in the early 1950s.

The Lexington Apartment and Motor Inn was designed and built for the comfort of the traveling public. It offered large suites, televisions, telephones, a pool, and washer and dryer facilities. Some locations had fully equipped meeting rooms. The Lexington Inn was located on I-20 West in Fort Worth. The company operated 18 more locations in Texas. (Courtesy Tarrant County Archives.)

This is a postcard of the Venetian Room of the Holiday Inn. This facility offered live music for the entertainment of its guests. (Author's postcard.)

Construction on a new luxury hotel, the Americana & Tandy Center, was announced in July 1979, and the hotel opened for the public in 1981. The 508-room hotel and convention center was developed and owned by the Bass brothers. It is located on Main Street, close to Sundance Square, and crosses over Houston Street. An 18-foot opening in the building allows for traffic to pass through. The hotel incorporated new air-conditioning and heating technology. Reclaimed heat was used to warm the water used in the hotel. It also featured a 1,000-seat ballroom, balcony rooms, and a three-level parking garage. The hotel was built on the same spot that the city's first telephone exchange once stood.

The hotel was extensively renovated for $19 million in 1993. Renamed the Worthington, it now has a 1,000-seat ballroom. In 1995, the hotel received a four-star rating and currently operates as the Renaissance Worthington Hotel. It is known for its Christmas banquets (above). The photograph below shows the front desk mural of the Worthington. (Both, author's photograph.)

Although the Ashton Hotel opened in 2000, it is located in a 1915 building at the corner of Main and Sixth Streets. The Ashton, a 39-room luxury boutique property, is adjacent to the two-story Winfree building, which was constructed in 1890. An example of the urban renew of Fort Worth, the six-story Ashton building was remodeled for $9 million and is listed in the National Register of Historic Places. (Both, author's photograph.)

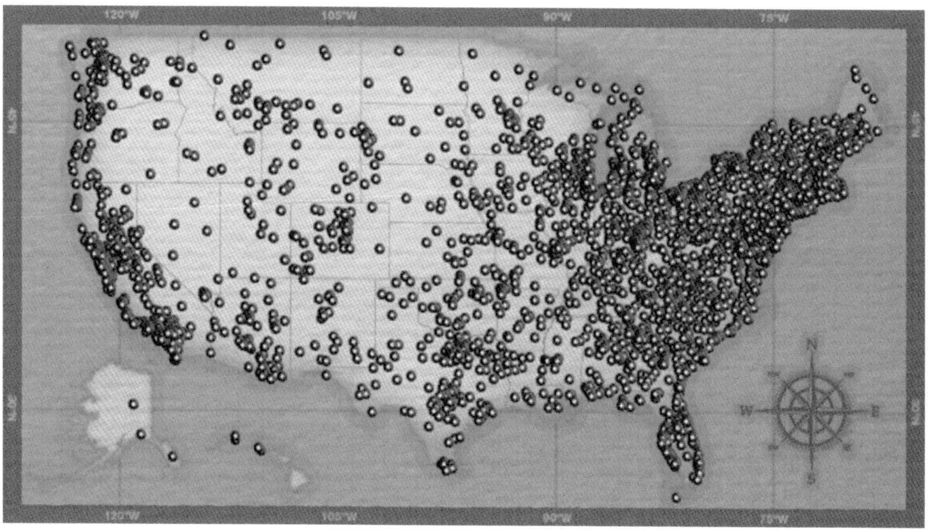